brave new mama

Vicki Rivard

Cover Design by
Emma Woodman | 21bcreative.com

Editing Support (and *Collector of Experiences* Term) by
Laura Burns | lauraburns.ca

(He)Art Support by
Laura Interlandi | birdsongbrooklyn.com

For Félix,

the blue sk'eyed boy
who started it all.

(I have loved you all of my lives.)

Foreword

New motherhood is a shot of adrenaline to the heart. It is a perfect prayer. It is mundane and magical. It is waking up to the wisdom in our marrow and laughing at the cosmic joke that we know absolutely nothing.

Several realities play themselves out at once on the inner landscape of a new mother. Meanwhile, she is often hidden from society and—let's be honest—far too tired to adequately explain the miraculous and painstaking labyrinth she has suddenly found herself living within.

In *brave new mama*, my friend and favourite heart healer, Vicki Rivard, generously takes our hand through this wild and turning garden maze, pointing out the delicate flowers, the individual songbirds, the rich earthen path below, and the roll of thunder in the distance.

As a post-partum doula, I do a number of things during each doula shift, ranging from preparing nutritious food that is easy to eat bleary-eyed and one-handed, to guiding a new mother through a relaxing visualization to help her ground down into her body and release the adrenaline of birth. Each small action is a calling up of the truth of what is happening, the magnitude of the moment, the rich and hearty work of life, recognized for what it is and given the support it is due.

At times, these offerings are received with delight while, at other times, it is like an awkward bumbling, trying to reconnect someone to the notion that they are still a person in the scenario, worthy of food and laughter and, yes, praise.

The more I sit with women and watch them shapeshift from maiden to mother, the more I feel a deep and shared ancestral wound, where the honouring of the guts of our matriarchs should be.

I see smart, talented, and conscious women subjected to mass cultural gaslighting; capable, wise women cowering in the shadows of societal expectations, often with little or no real support to meet them. The truth is that these expectations can never be met, and that constant feeling of failure is its own sublimated system of oppression that we must resist. One way we can do that is by validating and celebrating ourselves and each other.

This little book is not only the perfect gift to tuck into a baby shower basket, it is a **vital** contribution to our collective rising up, to the much-needed shift humanity is calling for. It is both a deeply intimate nod to each woman who reads it, as well as an impassioned battle cry, *"Look at us! Look at what we do with our bodies and our hearts and our brave brave souls! We are building a new world, we are birthing the resistance. Our love will heal humanity."*

One of the most difficult aspects of my job is walking out the door. Because the work is never done. Mothering is never done. Ever. Therefore, opportunities to support the mother, the parents, are unending. While the immense impact of intersectional circumstance can greatly vary individual experience, the relentless devotional unfurling of the first year is universal. Every mother deserves to be held heart-to-heart.

I often wish, as I am leaving a new mother's home, that I could leave a piece of myself behind to continue the work after I am gone.

Now, I can.

The *brave new mama* poems are like tiny doulas, each one bringing food and foot rubs for the soul, all the while softly illuminating the blurred stacks of feelings that new motherhood leaves daily on the doorstep.

Between the lines, a lullaby sings, *"You are okay. You are strong. I see you. You are doing holy work."*

I am deeply grateful for the medicine of these words, for myself and those I serve. Thank you, Vicki, for giving a voice to the Brave New Mama in all of us.

Laura Interlandi, PCD (DONA)
Doula and Educator
Co-Founder Birdsong Brooklyn

the poems
press
against your skin.

open your pores.

let them in.

— motherhood is poetry

the barrier broke &
there
was the baby
carried on the current &
there
were the word-waves
crashing.

— birth

it was when she placed him on my chest
that i finally knew myself —
my place
my purpose
my power
here.

— the first

i journeyed to the edge & back &
now i know
i know
i know:

1.   the first breath is sacred.
       the last one is, too.

2.   we are here
       for a mere moment.

3.   long ago, you chose me.
       long ago, i chose you.

— may 2, 2015 at 12:17am

this tendril of

i
n
f
i
n
i
t
y

unfurling from
the depths of me.

i catch
          my breath.

                    my breath

                              catches me,

                                        barely.

— love & the falling into it

bruised
bloodied
lying here
feeling it —
the exquisite pain
of being done,
of having just begun.

— i, wide open

at first,
it was clumsy,

an awkward two-step
of head & heart.

but we practiced &
we practiced

until
it was easy,

until
it was honey,

until
it was home.

— feed

i can't come to the door, i said.
i have seven pounds of stardust
resting on my chest.

— priorities

rocking to sleep
a newborn babe
is a prayer for peace
on earth.

— the rocking chair & the beating heart

this house is a temple now.
the neighbours don't know but
this house is a temple now.
the miracles are here.

— innes avenue

do not be misled
into thinking
you should be doing more.

rest.
feed.
heal.
hold.
feel.

these are the seeds.
the beginning.
be gentle with it all.

— holy days

it was epic & i have grown from it.

it was epic & i have grown from it.

— conversation between
a vaginal birth mama & a c-section mama
(when a woman is empowered)

my body
bleeds
the earth
crimson.

i empty
so much of me
to make space for
so much of you.

— the fourth trimester

boil the bones. drink.
you must unhollow yourself somehow.

— broth

bless the friends who
bring the food.

— the casseroles kept us warm

be patient
with your healing self.

be gentle
with your patience.

— time & tenderness

this is a forever thing.
      a forever soft thing.
            a forever soft surrender thing.

— this mothering thing

you are allowed
to feel blessed & bitter
bewildered & bruised
to stand in wonder
heart-deep in wounds
touching the sweet spot of
total bliss,
unravelled &
weeping
weeping.

— you are allowed all of it

i looked in the mirror &
recognized a mother's face.

there it was, pooling in my eyes,
all of that love &

yes, yes, there it was too —

grace.

— aria | for laura

the baby rocks the mother too.
her whole world,
in fact.

— epicenter

this life,
        it is so
        little now.

this little life,
        it is so
        big.

— big little things

it seems awfully unfair to
keep all of that extra weight &
lose all of that extra hair.

— hormones

they will ask,
how is it &
you will know not
what to say
because
joy
love
sadness &
surrender
are swimming
on your tongue.
so you will say,
it is everything
it is everything &
they will walk away.

(but those who stay
oh, those who stay.)

— the inner circle
        (it gets smaller, it gets stronger)

tiny hands
touch
my face,
trace
my lines,
turn
my features
into braille.

that he may know me
anywhere
everywhere,
that he may find me
even in
especially in

the dark.

— memorization

a sleep-deprived mama
is a fragile
ferocious
thing.

— handle with care

loving like this —
let it break you like
the sun breaks the night,
rising above, spilling
light.

— daybreak

i gave birth
to a whole universe.

— eyes

i look at him & see
the forgotten parts of me —
the sea skin i was born in
rose petals in my feet
fire mind, burning curious
winged heart, wild
free.

— how we begin

he cannot help
but be a poem.
he is the perfect thing.

— my boy

i strive to be
earthlike,
sturdy & stable,
though the spinning —
it is constant.

— terra firma

i leaned into the
ancient oak & asked,
how
how
how &
heard the root say,
hold on &
heard the leaf say,
let go &
heard the hundred year-old heartwood say,
go slow
go slow
go slow.

— what the tree told me

trust your heart.

— there is no textbook

[but if you can't hear your heart today,
trust the tree, on page 40.]

you thought you knew
but you didn't know
did you.

(i thought i knew too.)

how could we know.
how could we know.
how could we know.

there is no knowing
that the mother
is a lion
until the daughter
becomes a lion
herself.

— if i had known
        (i would have been kinder to my mother)

here,
you will lose yourself &

here,
you will find yourself &

here,
you will reveal yourself to yourself.

— here, in the wilderness of your becoming

there is moonlight in my skin.
i see it in me because
i see it in him.

— beaming

1. rub her feet.
2. pour her a bath.
3. tell her she is beautiful. (do this often.)
4. come home early.
5. feed her well. (her heart, especially.)

— reminders for the partners

the roses in your chest will wither.
feed the soil.
find the sunlight.
follow the water &
wait &
wait &
know
that
the roses in your chest will bloom
again
tomorrow.

— garden

some will
turn away
when you show them
your bleeding.
some will
stay.
will press stars
into the wounds.
will hold your feet
as you learn
to walk again
with the weight
of a too-full heart
pummelling
your bones.

— healers

i must

unshackle myself from
the harsh voices,

plunge deep
into my
gut &

trust

that i can mother
from there
instead.

— gutsong

take this heart
for a moment.
it is too full of sun.
i need a cool drink. rest.
i need to catch my breath.

— feelings

my softness is an ocean,
deep
warm &
rising.

— the (m)other kind of global warming

maybe today
was an easier day &
maybe you feel like,
i've got this
i've got this.

maybe tomorrow
will be the hardest day yet &
maybe you'll feel like
you're drowning.

but maybe tomorrow
you'll remember today &
maybe you'll whimper,
i've got this
i've got this.

(a whimper is a roar
submerged
just a little.)

— swimming lessons

we hold each other
tight & up.

— marriage | for yves (brave new papa)

i did not know
i could love like this &
i did not know
that i did not know.

— the great awakening

there will be dark days.
days when the rays
don't reach
past your curtains &
the deep blue
ink-stains
your bones.

— the heavy

but there will be feather days, too.

— the light

i am struck
daily
by the vast
deserts
between
mothers.
by the way
we avert
our eyes from
our eyes.
by the way
we long
to speak
from deep inside
our bones
but speak
instead
from the surface of
our skin.

— parched
(find the ones who are water &
call them *sisters*)

i hope you find your sisters.
the ones who will ask,
how beats your heart.
where are you breaking.
what are you aching to say.

— sisters 1

i hope you find your sisters.
the ones who will say,
show me your truth.
share of your struggle.
trust that your story is safe.

— sisters 2

i hope you find your sisters.
the ones who will not say
anything at all
but gift you
with presence,
with silence,
with

space.

— sisters 3

mother + hood

— it takes a village

when deep in doubt. in sadness. in fear. in shame.
in love. in heartache. in pain. breathe. breathe.
breathe. breathe. breathe. breathe. breathe. breathe.

— the breath will set you free

the heart is one.
she is only one.
but oh,
what hope
she holds.
what power
she pulsates.
what magic
she makes
in the world.

— the mighty one | for the single mamas

earth holds your feet.
you are held
firmly
by the land
that loves you.

— you are held
        (remember this)

sex after birth.
it's complicated.
i fear
my vagina
will swallow my husband whole &
he will end up
lost
somewhere
floating amongst stars.

— portal

i reach
my hand
inside
my beautiful
tattered heart,

sift through a thousand
beating fragments of
a difficult human life &

pick out
courage

— before sunrise

follow your love.
it knows the way.

— thump-thump-thump

i forget sometimes
in the foggy-headed
zombie moments
of the night
that
i've got the moon
i've got the stars
i am not alone.

— good company

my mother's hands
are in my hands.
we hold it together
together.

— lineage | for my mama & my mama's mama

breastmilk & life.
sticky & sweet.

— motherhood, too

sun.
son.
same.

— bright light

baby, slow down.
your smell —
it is fading.

— six months

i am body-tired but
i am spirit-strong.

— onwards

a challenge:

stay open.
in a world that wants to
zip you up,
simply stay
open.

— eyes & hands & heart & mind

meditation is a practice.
medicine is a practice.
motherhood is a practice, too.

— perfect doesn't live here anymore

do not abandon yourself
in a forest of false yesses.
when the first thought is,
no
say,
no.

— boundaries

so much of
how we mother
is determined by
how we breathe.

are your lungs
soft today,
is your breath
easy, or
are you choking
on sky.

— breathwork

only when
you have mastered the art
of telling my liver
how to cleanse blood &
of telling my kidneys
how to filter water
will i allow you
to tell my heart
how to mother.

— to the ones who know it all

when the arms are full &
the fridge is empty,
a squirt of breast milk in
a cup of coffee.

— desperate times

shower, uninterrupted.

— bliss
        (sometimes self-care looks like this)

when a mother
somewhere
forgives herself
for being human,

earth
exhales
a little.

— breeze

i miss my old life &
i don't miss my old life at all.
at the same time.
in the same breath, even.

— duet

i am learning my baby.
i am love-weaving a world.

— when they ask,
      what are you doing today?

when you fall on your knees
(& you will, you will)
you may look down
at the crumbs &
curse the mess
or up at God &
fuck the rest.

— kitchen floor prayers

you do not need
to lose yourself
or prove yourself
in busyness.
you may sit
for hours,
days, whole nights
with a babe at your breast,

holding on
        to your heart,
letting go
        of your breath.

this is enough.
this is everything.

— this is how we soften

dancing. with my baby. in the kitchen. at midnight. alone. in the world. together.

— some moments sing

too much love is like saying
too much sky or
too much earth or
too much tender.

— there is no such thing

your discomfort
has fallen
at my feet.
please
please
pick it up.
tuck it in your pocket or
your eyes or
your throat.
turn away.
walk away.
i will not tiptoe
around your misplaced
humiliation.
i will not be shamed
now
or ever
for this.

— breastfeeding in public

lift your inner wrist
to your ear &
listen,
listen hard.

your pulse is speaking
through thin skin.
it throbs the truth.

listen.
      listen.

— pulse diagnosis, part 1

the truth is this:

you are enough.
you are enough.
you are enough.
you are enough.
you are enough.
you are enough.
you are enough.
you are enough.
you are enough.
you are enough.
you are enough.
you are enough.
you are enough.
you are enough.
you are enough.
you are enough.
you are enough.
you are enough.
you are enough.
you are enough.
you are enough.
you are enough.
you are enough.
you are enough.

you are enough.
you are enough.
you are enough.
you are enough.
you are enough.
you are enough.
you are enough.
you are enough.
you are enough.
you are enough.
you are enough.
you are enough &
  when you are trapped inside
  your own self-spun web of reasons why
  the other mothers
  are better mothers,
you are enough.
you are enough.
you are enough.
you are enough.
you are enough.
you are enough.
you are enough.
you are enough.
you are enough.
you are enough.
you are enough.

you are enough.
you are enough.
you are enough.
you are enough.
you are enough.
you are enough.
you are enough.
you are enough.
you are enough.
you are enough.
you are enough.
you are enough &
      when the ten thousand ways
      you have failed today
      lodge between your vertebrae,
      bending your backbone,
you are enough.
you are enough.
you are enough.
you are enough.
you are enough.
you are enough.
you are enough.
you are enough.
you are enough.
you are enough.
you are enough.

you are enough.
you are enough.
you are enough.
you are enough.
you are enough.
you are enough.
you are enough.
you are enough.
you are enough.
you are enough.
you are enough.
you are enough &
       when you hover between worlds:
       grace & guilt, courage & fear,
       the wanting to be there &
       the needing to be here,
you are enough.
you are enough.
you are enough.
you are enough.
you are enough.
you are enough.
you are enough.
you are enough.
you are enough.
you are enough.
you are enough.

you are enough.
you are enough.
you are enough.
you are enough.
you are enough.
you are enough.
you are enough.
you are enough.
you are enough.
you are enough.
you are enough.
you are enough.
you are enough.
you are enough.
you are enough.
you are enough.
you are enough.
you are enough.
you are enough.
you are enough &
      when you think,
      feel, know
      you aren't,
      you are then, too.

— pulse diagnosis, part 2
      (this is not a poem, it is a **promise**)

'tis a brave thing indeed
to be such a tender-hearted mama
in such a broken-hearted world.

— courage, dear heart

even the moon hides herself once a month.

— take a break (hide)

the hummingbird appears
in the middle of the humdrum

fluttering its fragile wings
fast, so fast

as the everyday unrolls itself,

drops its acorns
floats its clouds
grows its grass.

find the hummingbird
                  the subtle spark
in this unremarkable day.

find the magic.

say,
        s t a y.

— everything is illuminated

motherhood paints herself
all over my face,
in a shadow here &
a drooping there &
unplucked brows &
smile lines &
i grow ragged &
i grow gorgeous,
all at once.

— objet d'art

i am still a wild night.
i have not lost the fury.

— the woman

take it off.
look at you.
your landscape is glorious.

— mom bod

mothers must mother
each other, too.

we must hold each other up &
surround each other strong &
in the ear
of every new mother
we must whisper,
you belong
you belong.

— come together | for valentina

folie | madness:

the way it feels
to love &
to break
so profoundly &
so often.

— mother tongue 1

époustouflant | breathtaking:

the way he looks at me,
as though he knows me
as though he chose me.

(he does &
he did.)

— mother tongue 2

éphémère | fleeting:

this moment
this moment
this
      m
            o
                    m
                         e
                              .
                              .
                              .
                              .
                              .

(here for a heartbeat, in the ether forever.)

— mother tongue 3

we rest
skin against
skin,
our pores
conversing
in a language
all their own &
i think,
this world
needs more rest,
more skin against
skin.

— bare

my placenta is in my freezer still.
some days, i swear,
i can hear her singing.

— hallelujah

1. how to make art. any art.
2. how to befriend the lonely hearts.
3. how to play in the mud. (how to pray there, too.)
4. how to stay curious.
5. how to stay kind.

— things i want to teach my boy

those moments —
the ones so full
of water,
when a mama &
her baby
are flooded
by the feel of
the warm
blood bond
that pours
out of the one
into the other &
back again
like a rolling
river, forever
flowing its way
home.

— source

i hold him
close enough
to kiss him &
yet
i miss him.
i miss him.
i miss him.

— the cord

there is the
stretching of
skin &
there is the
stretching of
heart.

only one is temporary.

— heartmarks

because i know
how to carry
ocean in my body.

because i know
how to bleed
life into the ground.

because i know
how to sing
fear into the fire.

because i know
how to hip sway
moon into the morning.

— because of this & so much more
                    (i know how to mother)

my arms have
softened into
feathers.
my words have
sweetened into
song.

— bird

someday
my boy will ask,
why is there war in the world.

i will not have an answer &
i wonder,
how does a mother mother, sometimes.

these —
the things that keep me up at night
when the baby doesn't.

— the tough questions

oh, how she tugs
so persistently
at the frayed hem
of my heart.

— life

i can't see the stars
tonight
or any night
but they are there
guiding me back home
to myself.

— toronto skies

you may not have
picked up
a pen or
a paintbrush
in weeks or
months
but
this
is
(he)artwork, too.

this
is
the deepest
(he)artwork
you'll ever do.

— creativity

you will not believe me but
believe me:

your fire is showing.
your fierce.
your fight.
your extraordinary light.

— to the woman with tired eyes & leaky breasts &
        tangled hair & screaming babe
                in front of me in line
                        at loblaws
                                (i see you)

1. find the water.
2. float.

— when the heart is heavy

forgive yourself with flowers,
blossomed by sun,
softened by rain.

wildflower yourself &
begin again.

— befriend yourself

my dreams have shrunk
from supernova
to speck.

but there is more light, here
(on this page)
than there ever was, there
(on that stage).

— changes

in this difficult world
there is a woman
there is a child &
there is a saltwater love
that softens the hardness
of all the raging wars, so
there is a harbour &
there is a healing
in this difficult world.

— the haven

let go
       like the shore
lets go
       of the ocean:

           eternally trusting
           in the homecoming.

— a mama must hold on, then a mama must let go
                        let grow
          her outside heart

there is the falling in love, yes.

but then
but then

there is the rising —

the rising into
knowing faith &
knowing God &
knowing the miraculous exists because
your own body birthed it &

you feel it
you feel it

in everything you do &
in every moment that undoes you.

— ascension

those feelings —
the ones that do not fit
inside my mouth.
maybe
they are not meant
to be named
at all.
maybe
they are meant
to be known
by heart
alone.

— i place my hand on my heart & know

i will soft mother my way through.

— sensitivity

i feel it
all
all
all
all
all
all
all &
still
i choose
to love
the world &
still
i choose
to trust
the love.

— love over fear | for noa

the art
of stitching your own
heart
back together
again.

& again & again & again & again & again & again
& again & again & again & again & again & again
& again & again & again & again & again & again
& again & again & again & again & again & again
& again & again & again & again & again & again
& again & again & again & again & again & again
& again & again & again & again & again & again
& again & again & again & again & again & again
& again & again & again & again & again & again
& again & again & again & again & again & again
& again & again & again & again & again & again
& again & again & again & again & again & again
& again & again & again & again & again & again
& again & again & again & again & again & again
& again & again & again & again & again & again
& again & again & again & again & again & again,

forever.

— mend

we stand
upon the shoulders
of every mother
who has come before.

these are the giants.
the forgotten heroes.
the beating hearts who
bled us all into
beating hearts of our own.

may we etch their wisdom
into our palms,
weave their stories
into our prayers &
may we make them proud.

— unsung

my veins, those lifelines —
they tremble with
truth.

— the knowing that lives in our girlblood

come closer
sister sister
so i may whisper
in your ear,
you are still here.
you are still here.

— to the one who feels invisible today

this life
is the quiet
revolution.

like
the atom
the air &
the answer,

unseen,
not unimportant.

— there are a thousand ways to rise

i am all of the mothers
i have ever met.

— pieces

i loved you
a thousand years ago.
i have loved you
all of my lives.

— the return

maybe
someday
my boy
all grown
will find the book
will read the words
will think,
my mama loved me
will know,
my mama loved &
maybe
this is
why i write.

— ~~maybe~~ love is the poem

don't blink, they said.

i blinked.

(don't blink.)

— one year

brave
      is in the bone.
new
      is in the blood.
mama
      is in the beat-after-beat-after-beat of her
growing
aching
tender
praying
loving
breaking
lion
heart.

— brave new mama | for all of us

Afterword

Sister. Hi. Here you are.

You have read the book, perhaps in one sitting or, perhaps, in pieces scattered across many days and nights. You have given it your time (though you may not have much of this) and your attention (though you may not have much of this, either) and I am grateful.

How are you? How is your heart? Do you feel seen? Held? Lifted?

The words in this book were born simply out of a need to make space inside of myself for all of the love (and all of the other feelings) that come with new motherhood.

However, as I wrote and re-wrote the pieces—and as I shared them with other mothers (with you)—I started to feel something like a fire, inside. A burning. An ancient flame, glowing brighter and warmer with each word, each breath, each time another mother said, *"me too, me too"* and, *"thank you, thank you."*

I started to sense that I was touching something special, here. Reclaiming something sacred.

I started to know that the book was less about *me* and more about *us*.

The widespread disregard for mother's voice, mother's intuition, and mother's wisdom is a desperate attempt, by a fading system, to erase the magic we are made of.

But here is the thing about magic: it can never be erased. It can be displaced. It can be forgotten, for awhile. But it is always there, shimmering in our eyes, begging to be remembered.

New motherhood—by its sheer rawness, its complete stripping of all that is not soul—carries with it immense potential to shake us into remembering both the magic in ourselves, and the magic in each other.

But most of us, while navigating the first year of holding one's heart outside of one's body, are too tired to remember. We are too immersed in the daily to-dos. We are too tender. We fear we are throbbing out of ourselves.

As I worked on the book and connected, on a soul-level, with other tired, tender, throbbing mothers, I tapped into the deeper and truer purpose of this work—that of gently rocking us awake, of guiding us back, word by word, to our remembering.

This remembering is the magnetic force that pulls us together, in joy and pain and a shared understanding of our vastly different, yet vastly similar, journeys.

This remembering is the surging sea water that spills out of our stories, softening our world for our babies and our babies' babies.

This remembering is the balm that heals our heart and the medicine song that honours our lineage.

My wish is that the words contained in this little book help to bring you back to your miraculous self, especially in those moments when the fog of sleep-deprivation has you asking, *"who am I, again?"*

May the words become friends. May you visit them often. May they be a mirror reflecting all of your light back to you—all of your purpose, all of your power, all of the magic you are made of.

We are the mothers we have been waiting for.

We are tired. We are tender. But we are awake.

I see you.
I see you.
I see you.

I remember.

Vicki Rivard
Callander, ON

Thank you, Gabriel.

(The love we carry will carry us home.)

About the Writer

Vicki Rivard is a collector of experiences. She has dedicated chapters of her life to studying, acting, travelling, teaching, and, most recently and blessedly, mothering. Writing is the thread that holds her together.

Her words have been published in Reader's Digest, elephant journal, Sacred Pregnancy, Rebelle Society, and on her blog, The Wellness Way.

In 2017, Vicki lost a baby in the 18th week of pregnancy. This loss—of her son, Gabriel—is what propelled her to publish this book, which she wrote during the first year of mothering her firstborn son, Félix.

Vicki practices Traditional Chinese Medicine and Holistic Nutrition and is a fierce advocate for the healing of this planet and its people. In 2013, she was awarded the Karen Haffey Memorial Award for Leadership in Changing the World by the Institute of Traditional Medicine in Toronto, Canada.

Vicki believes in the connection between all beings, in the body's innate ability to heal, and in the transformative power of nature, words, and love.

She was once reminded, by a deer in the forest, to "*keep believing in the magic,*" so she does.

She currently lives in Callander, Ontario with her family.

Connect with her at her website (www.vickirivard.com) and follow her on Instagram (@vicki_rivard | @bravenewmama) and/or on Facebook (/vjr26).

82267348R00088

Made in the USA
Columbia, SC
09 December 2017